D1273769

DATE DUE			

616.2
ISL

30408000000576
Isle, Mick.

**Everything you need
to know about colds
and flu**

Lexile: 1052

**Woodland High School
Henry County Public Schools**

752467 02095   52399A   0023

Everything You Need to Know About Colds and Flu

Woodland High School
800 N. Moseley Dr.
Stockbridge, GA 30281
770-389-2784

Colds and flu can make you miserable, but try to remember that everyone gets them.

Everything You Need to Know About Colds and Flu

Mick Isle

The Rosen Publishing Group, Inc.
New York

*To Helen, who made rose hip tea, boiled the soup, brought the Jed,
wrote the notes, and cared.*

Published in 2000 by The Rosen Publishing Group, Inc.
29 East 21st Street, New York, NY 10010

Copyright © 2000 by The Rosen Publishing Group, Inc.

First Edition

All rights reserved. No part of this book may be reproduced in any
form without permission in writing from the publisher, except by a
reviewer.

Library of Congress Cataloging-in-Publication Data

Isle, Mick.
    Everything you need to know about colds and flu / by Mick Isle.
        p. cm. (The need to know library)
Includes bibliographical references and index.
Summary: Explains what both colds and flu are, how to avoid them, and
how to get over an illness as quickly and painlessly as possible.
    ISBN 0-8239-3297-4
    1. Cold (Disease)—Juvenile literature. 2. Influenza—Juvenile lit-
erature. [1. Cold (Disease). 2. Influenza. 3. Diseases.] I. Title II. Series.
    RF361 .I84 2000
    616.2'03—dc21

                                                       00-008572

Manufactured in the United States of America

Contents

Introduction

Some things about winter are really great: If you live in a cold climate you can ski, toboggan down steep hills, and come out of the cold to a nice cup of steaming hot chocolate. If you live in a warm climate, winter brings you clear, sunny skies, no need for air conditioning, and no snowstorms. However, some things about winter are not so great at all: having to get out of a warm bed when it's still dark; cars that splash slush all over your clothes; coming down with a bad cold or a miserable case of the flu.

Unfortunately, unless you are lucky enough to live in balmy Hawaii or Southern California, it is somewhat of a miracle if you get through an entire winter season without catching one or the other virus. And frequently, you can end up catching both.

The funny thing about both colds and the flu is that even though basically everybody gets them, most people don't know that much about them. For instance, many people are clueless as to how to keep from getting the flu in the first place. Others have no idea of which medicines to take—or not to take—to get over a cold quickly. Still others don't even know whether what they have is a cold, a case of the flu, or something else entirely different.

Surprisingly—for two such common ailments—there are many myths and misconceptions with respect to both colds and flu. This book will help you learn what exactly both colds and flu are, and how to avoid them. If, however, you are unlucky enough to come down with one or the other, this book will tell you how to get over your illness as quickly and painlessly as possible.

Fever and chills are typical cold and flu symptoms.

Chapter One

What Exactly Are Colds and Flu?

*I*t was in the middle of biology when Paolo realized that he was feeling hot. He ran the back of his hand across his forehead and was surprised to find it moist with sweat. Maybe the heat was turned up too high. Paolo leaned over and opened the window a bit. A blast of frosty, winter air leaked into the classroom. Paolo felt better, but his lab partner, Ginny, shot him a dirty look. "Shut the window, loser," she commanded, scowling. "We're in the middle of winter!"

Because Paolo was a little afraid of Ginny—and because he wanted to be able to keep copying her lab reports—he shut the window. Still feeling hot, he took off his sweater instead. Ginny arched her eyebrows. *"Trying to show off your muscles?"* she snorted.

Ten minutes later, Paolo decided to put on his sweater. Not because Ginny's snide comment had made him self-conscious about his muscles—or lack of them—but because he was practically shivering with cold. It seemed as if chilly fingers were creeping up his back. And his head felt sort of woozy, too.

"Why are you so sweaty?" asked Ginny with disgust in her voice. *"Didn't you take a shower after gym class?"*

"I'm not feeling so good," moaned Paolo, putting his head down on the lab table. *"I feel all achy and cold and these fluorescent lights are hurting my eyes."*

"Oooo! Get away from me!" hissed Ginny, as she scraped her chair as far away as possible from Paolo. *"It sounds like you have the flu. And I, for one, don't want to catch it!"*

By the time biology was over, Paolo felt so lousy he didn't even want to stay at school. He went to the nurse's office and told her his symptoms. *"My throat feels kind of itchy, too,"* he confessed.

"Yes, it sure does sound like the beginnings of the flu to me," said the nurse sympathetically. She wrote out a sick slip so that Paolo could leave school early. *"Go home, get into bed, and drink*

plenty of liquids," said the nurse. "If you take good care of yourself, you should be better in a few days."

Paolo wasn't too happy to hear Ginny's prediction confirmed. He hated being sick. There was a bright side, however—at least, he wouldn't have to put up with Ginny for a few days.

Both colds and flu are contagious viral infections that attack the respiratory system. Viruses are extremely simple microscopic organisms. They are almost like very tiny, tiny bugs—this is why people often refer to "flu bugs" or talk about catching a certain "bug" that's going around—that grow and multiply in living cells. Contagious viruses are ones that spread very easily, passing diseases—sometimes very serious ones—from one person to another. Flu viruses are particularly contagious. It is estimated that at least 90 million Americans come down with the flu every year!

The Common Cold

The common cold is the perfect name for this viral infection that each year gets so many noses running and lungs coughing. First of all, it is very common. Secondly, it tends to rear its sneezy head during the chilliest months of the year.

Colds can be brought on by a number of common viruses—200 of them, in fact. The most common of all

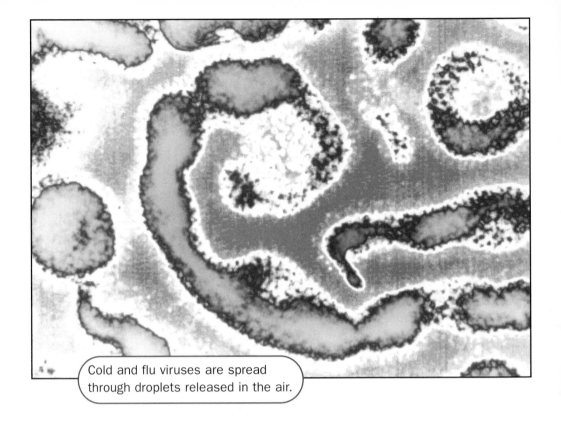

Cold and flu viruses are spread through droplets released in the air.

are rhinoviruses and coronaviruses. These viruses attack the respiratory system and end up affecting your nose, throat, sinuses, and ears.

Colds attack basically everybody. But kids—especially young ones—seem to be favorite victims of the virus, probably because classrooms, auditoriums, hallways, and school buses are great places to pass the virus from one kid to another. The way you get a cold is by breathing in virus particles that are spread through the air when someone sneezes or coughs. You can also get it from kissing (the wetter the kiss, the more dangerous), shouting in someone's face, shaking hands (if you breathe on your hand beforehand, and your pal wipes his face with his hand afterward),

MYTH

Colds are not caused by cold, wet weather. Or by diving into a cold lake. Or by getting caught in a rainstorm. Or by working in an ice-cream parlor and leaning into the freezers too frequently. Colds are caused by viruses.

drinking from the same soda can, and so on. In short, you can get a cold from any kind of close person-to-person contact.

Influenza

Most generally known by its shorter nickname—"the flu"—influenza is an extremely common disease caught every year by billions of people all over the world. Like colds, flu tends to "go around" in winter and early spring and is especially widespread among kids. In fact, many flu epidemics—or large-scale outbreaks—begin in schools and then spread through the entire school community as students take the virus home with them to give to their families and neighbors. (Like colds, flu is spread from one person to another through droplets released when someone coughs or sneezes.) During serious epidemics, up to 50 percent of people in a given neighborhood can be found laid up in bed, downing herbal teas and staring bleary eyed at their television screens. To keep the spread of flu from getting really out of hand, community leaders might decide to close schools or cancel public meetings.

In actual fact, there isn't just one type of flu virus, but three. Type A spreads with the most ease and rapidity and boasts the most violent symptoms. Type B—with symptoms that are less severe—is responsible for smaller outbreaks, whereas Type C is a much milder and rarer strain of flu.

The other tricky thing about the flu is that from one year to the next, the virus that causes it is never the same. These yearly changes are very obnoxious for humans. This is because when we come down with a viral illness, our bodies have an automatic defense system that kicks in. It manufactures special proteins—called antibodies—that attack the virus and then stick around to make sure that the same virus can't harm you in the future. Flu viruses are wily, however, in that they change every year. Some years the change is so slight that even if you get the flu, it will be a very mild case because of the partial protection given by the previous year's antibodies. However, about every ten years, the virus undergoes a radical change and a great many people end up suffering from serious cases of flu. Sometimes, these flu epidemics are so severe that they spread worldwide. In such instances, you are no longer dealing with a flu epidemic but a flu pandemic—an outbreak of flu that spreads over a wide geographic area.

Pandemic Frenzy

The twentieth century has seen its share of influenza pandemics. There was the Hong Kong flu of 1968 and the Asian flu of 1957. However, the worst of all was the Spanish flu of 1918, which infected one-quarter of the U.S. population and one-fifth of the population of the world. It killed an estimated 20 to 40 million people worldwide! In the United States alone, this deadly strain of flu was responsible for the deaths of more people than World War I, World War II, the Korean, and Vietnam Wars combined!

The Spanish flu was particularly horrible. Those infected had so much liquid in their lungs that they literally drowned to death—with bloody fluid pouring out of their noses and flooding their bedsheets. There were so many people dying that cities were forced to use streetcars to transport dead bodies to mass graves that had been dug in a hurry.

Chapter Two

Not Getting Sick

Even though, at times, it seems that everybody is coming down with a cold or a case of flu, there are certain precautions you can take to prevent getting sick in the first place.

How to Play It Safe

The best way of not catching someone else's cold or flu virus is by staying out of his or her way. This means that if someone is showing obvious symptoms such as coughing or sneezing, don't get too close. Ask your best friend to cover her mouth when she coughs. Make sure that when your little brother coughs, he covers his mouth. Of course, the tricky thing is that people who catch a cold or flu become contagious long before the recognizable symptoms begin to appear. In the case of

16

A person can be contagious for several days before any symptoms appear.

both, it can take between two and four days before the obvious signs kick in.

So to play it safe, try to avoid crowds if one or the other virus is going around. Do not share drinking glasses (get your parents to buy some disposable paper cups for the bathroom) or bathroom towels. None of these methods will actually ensure that you don't come down with a bug, but they will diminish your chances of getting one.

Your Nose

Your nose has a much more important function than just sitting in the middle of your face. In fact, it is a sensitive instrument designed to filter out dust and germs from entering your body. When you breathe through your mouth, any bacteria or virus can just charge in and infect you, particularly your throat, bronchial passages, and lungs. But breathing through a clear, unblocked nose can diminish your chances of catching a cold or flu.

A Hands-Off Approach to Not Getting Sick

Two frequent ways that cold and flu viruses enter your body are via your nose and eyes. And just how do they accomplish this? Usually by your rubbing, scratching, touching, or poking them with your own virus-contaminated hands. Surprised that you would do such a thing to yourself?

Washing your hands frequently can eliminate many cold and flu germs.

Let's say you go to the corner store to buy some licorice. You hand the cashier a dollar bill. She hands you change. Then, with that same hand, you rub your eyes, which are tearing. Or you scratch your nose, which is itching. In doing so, all the potential germs from all the potential hands that may have touched either that dollar bill or that change are going straight into your eyes or nose.

There is an easy way not to infect yourself: Wash your hands—always—before touching your eyes or nose. This is a surefire way to get rid of germs that you might pick up by shaking hands, pressing elevator buttons, touching poles on a crowded bus, or borrowing a friend's pen. Some experts estimate that 80 percent of

> **MYTH**
>
> Eating nutritiously, exercising regularly, and getting the proper amount of sleep do not make you a less likely candidate for catching a cold or the flu. It does, however, mean that your body will be able to fight the virus more rapidly and efficiently than someone who is run-down, stressed-out, and flabby.
>
> Short of hiding out in your bedroom, jumping a plane for Brazil, or walking around in a plastic bubble, once you've taken the precautions mentioned above, there is, unfortunately, nothing you can do to prevent the onslaught of a cold. In terms of the flu, however, there exists a vaccine that has proved quite successful in keeping the virus at bay.

colds and flu could be eliminated by more frequent and thorough washing of your hands with soap and water.

Flu Shots

The flu vaccine, usually called a flu shot, protects people against the flu. In general, you can receive this injection between September and mid-November—right before the December–April flu season hits—although it is possible to get it at other times of the year as well.

A common myth about the flu shot is that it can actually cause the flu. However, in North America, the flu vaccine is made from killed influenza viruses. Because

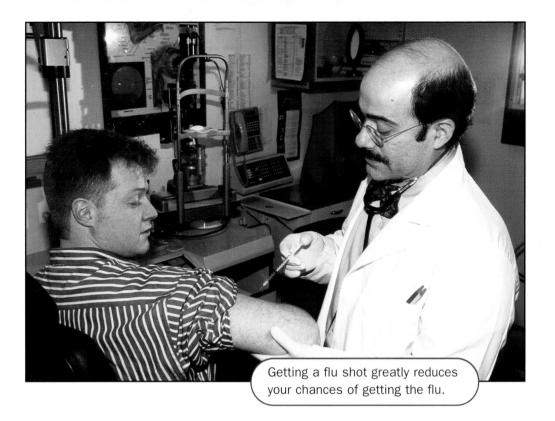

Getting a flu shot greatly reduces your chances of getting the flu.

the viruses are dead, it is impossible to catch the flu by getting a flu shot. The viruses injected into your upper arm will trigger your body to start making antibodies. This takes about a week or two. Should the real, live virus make an appearance, these antibodies will be all set to attack and destroy. The flu shot reduces your chances of getting the flu by 60 to 80 percent. But even if you do come down with the flu, your symptoms will be much less severe.

The reason flu shots aren't 100 percent sure is that—as we saw in chapter 1—the virus has a nasty habit of changing from year to year. Figuring out in advance what next year's virus will be—and manufacturing an appropriate vaccine—is a complicated task.

Flu vaccines are made by culturing the virus in chicken eggs.

How Flu Vaccines Are Made

Oddly enough, flu vaccines are made in chicken eggs! This is done by injecting a tiny droplet of the flu virus into an egg. Three days later, the original droplet has grown and can now fill a tablespoon. The virus is now ready. The tops of the eggs are chopped off and the virus is suctioned out. A major manufacturer might use up to 150,000 eggs at once to make 250,000 gallons of pure virus. Before it can be used, the vaccine must be purified, tested, approved by the Food and Drug Administration (FDA), packaged, labeled, and distributed.

What makes flu shots a bit of a gamble is that all of this takes at least six months. Because flu shots go "on sale" every fall, by springtime the vaccine-makers have to know which virus they will need to grow for the upcoming season. In February or March, the World Health Organization's (WHO) international team of flu experts begins collecting flu samples from patients. These samples are then sent off to laboratories to be tested. Strange and new strains of the virus are sent to be analyzed by the Center for Disease Control (CDC) in the United States, or to one of many National Influenza Centers around the world. The results of all these tests are given to vaccine-makers so that they can start making the upcoming year's flu shots. The problem is that sometimes, between the time the WHO makes its prediction and the time the vaccine is ready to be shot into your arm, the virus might have changed even more. This is why the vaccine is never 100 percent effective.

Whether or not you get a flu shot is up to you, your parents, and your doctor. Flu itself is not always dangerous, but some of its complications can be—especially for babies, little kids, older people, and those with certain health problems. For these reasons, most doctors recommend that people over age sixty-five and teens with medical conditions such as cystic fibrosis, asthma, heart disease, or sickle cell disease get the flu vaccine every year. Other teens who might benefit from the vaccine are those infected with the HIV virus or those with diabetes, kidney problems, or other chronic (long-term) medical conditions. If you live with someone in one of these high-risk groups, it might be a good idea to get vaccinated.

Cold feet cannot cause a viral infection but may undermine your immune system.

These days, getting a flu shot is easy. Hospitals, doctors' offices, school health clinics, pharmacies, community centers, and even some supermarkets all administer flu shots. After receiving a shot, you may experience a mild reaction for a day or so. This could range from feeling tired and feverish to having sore muscles or getting a light headache. Because the vaccine's viruses are grown in chicken eggs, anyone allergic to eggs or egg products should not get a flu shot. Others who should not get injected are healthy women in the early stages of pregnancy.

The Truth About Cold Feet

Some kids scoff when their parents start nagging at them not to walk around barefoot on a cold floor. After all, colds are caused by viruses, not by chilly kitchen tiles. However, there is some scientific truth to this old wives' tale. Although cold feet cannot produce a viral infection, they can undermine your body's defenses, thus increasing the chance of you getting sick.

Weirdly enough, there is a connection between your feet and your nasal passages. When your feet get frosty, the walls of your nasal passages become cold as well. They contract and grow dry and this stops the nasal glands from filtering out dust and germs and from creating the mucus that destroys cold germs. So whether you prefer socks, stockings, flip-flops, or slippers—keep your feet warm.

Chapter Three | Getting Sick

Let's say that you got your flu shot and you wash your hands constantly. In crowded places, such as buses and elevators, you wrap a bandanna around your nose and mouth to prevent breathing in germs. And when your girlfriend comes down with a cold, you both decide it is time to take a break from each other. Then, in spite of all your careful precautions, you wake up one morning with a runny nose and a sore throat and you realize that you're getting sick.

We all know that getting sick is no fun. In fact, depending on what's going on in your life at a specific point—a big exam, an important volleyball game, a ski trip, a long-awaited first date—it can be a big inconvenience. But as soon as you start feeling those telltale symptoms, do not ignore them. Follow the advice listed further on in this book and take serious care of yourself.

Some Chilling Statistics

- ◆ A cold is the number one reason that kids: 1) go to the doctor; 2) stay home from school.

- ◆ Some North American kids catch up to a whopping eight colds every year! (That's a fortune in cough drops and tissues.)

- ◆ The average cold makes you miserable for five to seven days.

Is It a Cold . . . or the Flu?

Susan felt just fine when she went to bed. Maybe she felt a little more tired than usual. Perhaps there was a slight itching in her throat. During the night, she slept like a rock. But when the alarm clock jolted her awake the next morning, Susan felt awful. Her head was throbbing and her throat was filled with mucus, which made her cough. She rubbed her watery eyes and felt her hot, sweaty forehead. "Oh no," she groaned out loud. "I've got a cold!"

However, two days later, after Susan's temperature had shot up to 104 degrees, her cough had

Colds and flu share many symptoms and are often mistaken for one another.

turned into a horrible hacking noise, and she felt so weak that she could barely make it to the bathroom, Susan's mom became worried and called Dr. Shawnie. "Doesn't sound at all like a cold to me," said Dr. Shawnie over the phone. "It sounds like a case of the flu, and a bad one at that. Susan should stay in bed, stay warm, and drink lots of liquids. If those symptoms don't improve over the next couple of days, or if they get worse, I want you to call me right away. We wouldn't want Susan to come down with a case of bronchitis or pneumonia."

Susan and her mom are not alone in mistaking the flu for a cold. Both illnesses are alike in many ways. Because both share many of the same symptoms, it is sometimes difficult to tell exactly what you've got, particularly in the beginning stages. In general, if you have a stuffy or

Common Symptoms of Colds and Flu

Symptom	Colds	Flu
Fever	Infrequent and low (99–100 degrees)	Very frequent. Can rise to 104 degrees and last for three to four days
Headache	Infrequent and mild	Very frequent
Body Aches and Pains	Minor	Frequent and often severe
Lack of Energy/ Weakness	Slightly Frequent	Can last up to two to three weeks
Extreme Exhaustion	Never	Early and often severe
Stuffed-up Nose	Frequent	Sometimes
Sneezing	Frequent	Sometimes
Sore Throat	Frequent	Sometimes
Cough	Frequent	Frequent, and can become severe
Chest Discomfort	Mild to moderate	Frequent

runny nose, a sore or itchy throat, and you are sneezing often, you have a cold. Tiredness, a fever, headaches and major aches, pains, and shivers are all signs that you have the flu. Coughing can be a sign of either a cold or the flu, but if it's a dry, hacking cough that makes you feel as if your insides are on fire, it's likely you have the flu.

Why We Sneeze

Cold viruses usually get to you via your nose. They move in, take over the cells lining your nostrils, and begin reproducing. To get rid of the invaders, your body dreamed up the sneeze. When your nerves detect a virus, they contact your lungs and get them to send a blast of air through your body. This blast—the Big Sneeze—comes "aaatchoo"-ing through your nose and blows those villainous viruses right out of your system. You probably didn't know that you can sneeze up to thirty miles an hour—the same speed as a car driving on a city street!

Mucus is the slimy, fluidlike substance inside your nose that usually becomes an often present nuisance during the cold. The reason that you seem to have an endless supply of mucus when you have a cold is that it acts as a powerful natural disinfectant, which destroys viruses. When you're sick, your immune system produces more mucus than usual. Whether propelled by the force of a sneeze, or running like a tiny river out of your nostrils, mucus expels the viruses out of your nose and prevents new viruses from entering.

Stomach flu is not really a type of flu but is actually gastroenteritis.

This means that being unable to stop sneezing is actually a sign that you are getting better.

What About Stomach Flu?

One day, Massimo left school feeling really rotten. His body felt all achy and sore and he had some strange cramps in his stomach. It helped to be out in the fresh air. During his last class he had been feeling increasingly nauseous, as if he was going to throw up. He wondered if it had been something he had eaten at lunch. He had traded his roast beef and potato chip sandwich for his friend Li's chop suey sandwich on a garlic bagel. But how could a sandwich be causing such bad cramps?

Massimo ran the last two blocks to his house. He opened the front door and ran straight upstairs to the bathroom, without even saying hi to his mom. Just in time, he thought, as he vomited into the toilet. Afterward, he went and flopped down on his bed. He felt horrible.

A few moments later, Massimo's mom knocked on the door. When Massimo groaned, she stepped inside and in a worried voice asked him what was wrong. "I think Li's mom poisoned me," Massimo moaned, after describing his symptoms. "Nonsense," said his mom. "A sandwich couldn't make you so sick, so fast. It sounds to me as if you have the stomach flu. Junie Rodrigues at the club said that her husband came down with a bad case last week. It must be going around."

Although it is contagious and can be caused by a virus—as well as bacteria and parasites—stomach flu isn't really a form of influenza. Its real name is gastroenteritis. Instead of affecting your lungs and respiratory system, this bug gets you right in the gut.

The bad news is that there is no vaccine for gastroenteritis. Once you get it, between vomiting and diarrhea, you'll be lucky if you can keep anything in your system. In fact, you shouldn't even try. The best remedy is to get plenty of bed rest and drink lots of mild, clear liquids. Liquids such as tea, broth, and ginger ale (the flatter, the better) will keep your stomach soothed and your body from dehydrating after losing so many natural fluids.

The good news is that gastroenteritis rarely lasts more than a day or two. However, if these symptoms do persist, you should definitely pay a visit to the doctor to ensure that you don't need antibiotics. When you have gastroenteritis, it is important that you stay close to the bathroom and that if you are going to try to eat, you eat bland, nonfibrous foods such as white bread, eggs, and rice.

Chapter Four

When You Become Very Sick

*I*t was Saturday afternoon and Lucas was pleased to note that his flu finally seemed to be going away. Even though his mom had said he should rest until he was completely better, after five days of being wrapped up in bed like an Egyptian mummy, he was dying to get out of the house. When his mom left for her karate class, Lucas called up his best bud Parker.

"Hey, Parker!" he yelled into the phone. "Let's round up some guys and play tackle football in the snow!"

"OK," said Parker. "But aren't you still sick?"

"Who are you calling sick? Truth is, I haven't felt this good in over a week. Still got a bit of a

34

cough, but some fresh air and exercise are just what the doc would prescribe."

Lucas got dressed up in his winter gear and went to meet Parker at the park. Just walking to the park made him feel kind of weak and breathless. He must have gotten seriously out of shape from having been cooped up so long. Playing football with Parker and the guys made him feel hot and sweaty, but he figured it was from running around in all of those warm clothes. Lucas also got out of breath very quickly. He found himself gasping for air and wheezing. At one point he had a violent coughing fit, during which he coughed up some yellow goop laced with a tinge of blood. It looked really gross in the white snow.

"Lucas, that's some scary stuff you're coughing up," said one of the guys.

"You should go home right away, dude," said another guy. "You're gonna contaminate us."

"Luke, I don't think you're better at all," said Parker in a concerned voice. "In fact, it looks like you're getting worse."

Parker took Lucas home. Lucas was feeling so weak that he had to put his arm around Parker's shoulder. A couple of times they had to stop because Lucas was seized with a coughing fit. When they got to Lucas' house, Lucas' dad was just getting home

Cold and flu symptoms can develop into serious illnesses.

from his karate class. He took one look at his son, doubled over and gasping for breath, and ordered him into the car. "We're going straight to see Dr. Ferreira," he said, turning the key in the ignition.

Dr. Ferreira gave Lucas a physical examination. "Well, your flu has taken a turn for the worse," said the doctor. "Looks like you've got a case of pneumonia." To calculate how serious the pneumonia was, Dr. Ferreira ordered blood tests and an X-ray of Lucas' chest. Then he sent both the patient and his dad home with a prescription for antibiotics and a warning for Lucas to drink plenty of liquids and get lots of rest.

"Guess that means no more tackle football in the snow for awhile," said Lucas.

The average cold lasts for a few days—a week, at most. Afterward, for another week, you might still have a bit of a runny nose and experience the odd cough. Flu lasts longer. The first two to three days, you'll usually experience fever and aches. These symptoms usually disappear after a few days, giving way to a sore throat, a stuffed-up nose, coughing, and fatigue. The cough and tiredness could last for a week or even two.

For a healthy teen, the run-of-the-mill cold or flu is no big deal. A few days of misery and then it's done. There is no need to get a doctor involved. If however, your symptoms take a sudden turn for the worse; last an unusually long time; or if, like Lucas, after feeling a little better, you develop signs of a more serious problem; you should definitely—and immediately—get checked out by a doctor. You might have developed either bronchitis, pneumonia, or a sinus infection—serious illnesses that, if left untreated, can even prove fatal.

Serious Symptoms

- Feeling sick to your stomach
- Throwing up
- High fever
- Shaking chills
- Chest pains
- Shortness of breath
- Coughing up thick yellow-green mucus

In teens, cases of pneumonia and bronchitis are less frequent and less serious than in adults over age 65 and little kids under the age of five. In fact, each year thousands of elderly people die from the flu or its complications, which is why doctors recommend that people in this age group get flu shots every year. Flu and its complications can also prove dangerous to the point of deadly to people who have received an organ transplant or people with AIDS. Such groups often have weakened

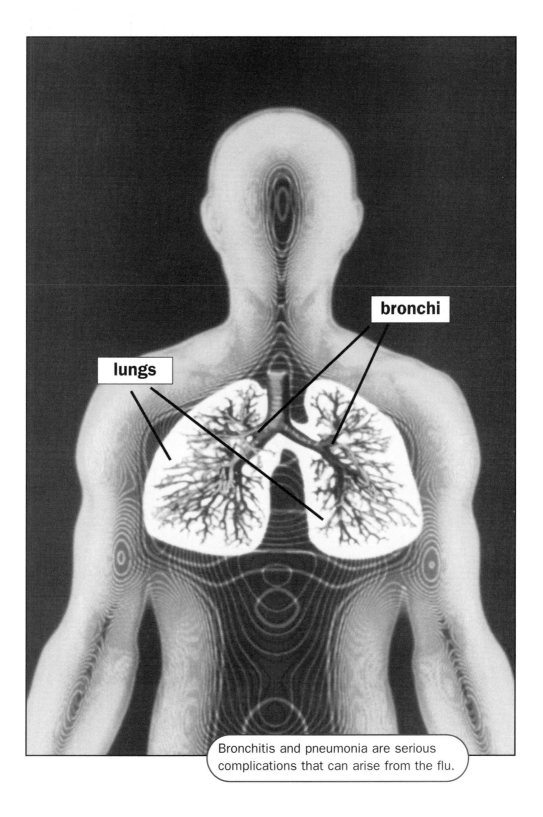

Bronchitis and pneumonia are serious complications that can arise from the flu.

immune systems, which makes it difficult for them to produce virus-fighting antibodies. Recent studies also suggest that pregnant women have an increased chance of developing serious complications from the flu.

Bronchitis

Four out of every 100 people come down with bronchitis each year. The virus usually shows up after the first symptoms of a cold or flu begin to wear off. It can be caused by a host of respiratory viruses which attack the respiratory system and cause the bronchi—the main air passages which lead to the lungs—to become infected.

Early signs that you might have developed bronchitis include a deep tickle in your throat that develops into a harsh, dry cough. As the infection progresses, you may begin coughing up thick yellow mucus, sometimes laced with blood. Other symptoms include chest pains, shortness of breath, wheezing, and fever. If treated properly—usually with antibiotics prescribed by your doctor—the worst of bronchitis is over in about a week to ten days. If things get worse (you begin coughing up blood or have trouble breathing) you might have acute bronchitis. This is serious and might require hospitalization.

Pneumonia

The other big, bad complication is pneumonia, which affects one in every 100 people each year. Pneumonia can be caused by bacteria, parasites, or viruses, including the flu virus, and is often a complication of flu. There are different categories of this lung-infecting disease, which can range in seriousness from mild to life threatening.

Pneumonia usually kicks in two to three days after initial cold or flu symptoms. Signs that you might have developed pneumonia include coughing up of greenish mucus, sharp chest pains, tiredness, a high fever, chills with shaking, headaches, nausea and vomiting, and an aching body. In severe cases, you might also experience excessive sweating, wheezing, shortness of breath, coughing up of blood, and abdominal pains.

People used to brag about having survived "double pneumonia." This commonly used old-fashioned term referred to cases of pneumonia in which both lungs had been infected. However, the fact is that just about all cases of pneumonia affect both lungs!

Like bronchitis, pneumonia can usually be cured by using prescribed antibiotics. In more serious cases, you might require oxygen as well as treatments that remove the fluids in your lungs. Most patients will get better within a period of two weeks.

Although many people are not aware of it, there exists a vaccine that works against the more common varieties of pneumonia. It is available year-round.

Chapter Five

Getting Better

Coming down with a cold or flu can be a pretty miserable experience. Bed can be a bore and there are only so many *Friends* reruns you can watch in one day. But there are two ways of dealing with your sickness: either you can let it get the best of you—or you can get the best of it. You might think that once the bug has got you in its grip, there is nothing you can do but sit in bed and wait for the cough, runny nose, and fever to pass. But if you choose to take charge of your cold or flu and show it who's the boss, you will get better much more quickly, suffer much less, and be able to return to your normal day-to-day life much sooner than you expected.

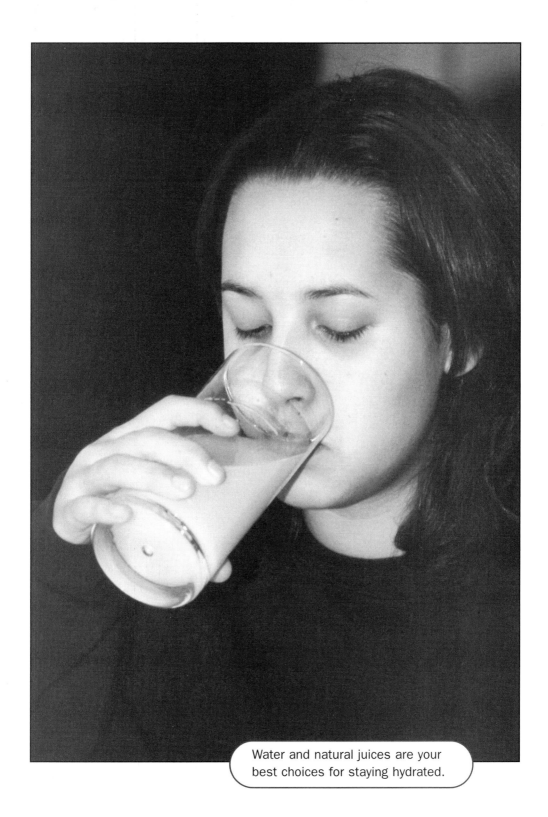

Water and natural juices are your best choices for staying hydrated.

The Basics

Everybody knows the basics about what to do when you have a cold or flu. Drink lots of fluids. Keep warm (lots of blankets, hot drinks, and extra socks). Do not exert yourself. Keep your hands clean. Stay home from school. Make sure to get plenty of rest; don't worry so much about missing classes. Chances are you wouldn't be very productive if you were there, and you would be exposing all your teachers and friends (and enemies, too) to the virus.

What to Drink

Drinking fluids all day long is very important. Liquids keep you hydrated and allow the viruses to pass more quickly out of your body. Water, which bolsters your immune system, as well as natural fruit and vegetable juices, are good choices. Orange, grapefruit, and tomato juice rule because they are full of vitamin C. Do not drink soft drinks —which actually deplete your body of water—and stay away from alcohol, which will dehydrate you. Anything with caffeine and/or sugar in it is not good because both undermine your immune system. Also, stay away from coffee. Drink only herbal teas. And sweeten hot beverages with honey instead of sugar. A particularly good hot remedy is to make tea using lemon juice, garlic, ginger and honey. And if you have a sore throat, frequent gargling with warm salty water should ease the pain.

Hot soup is soothing and provides needed nourishment.

What to Eat

Ignore the old saying: "Feed a fever, starve a cold." You are better off letting your appetite be your guide. If you are not hungry, do not force yourself to eat. You are better off getting your vitamins and energy from natural fruit and veggie juices. If you are hungry, try some hot soup, which will warm you up as well as provide nourishment. If your life's philosophy is "the hotter, the better," try seasoning your soup with any of the following spices: black pepper, cayenne pepper, chili pepper, or curry spices. In Latin cultures, where hot peppers are frequently used in cooking, bronchitis is virtually nonexistent. Eating cool, by contrast, is not at all cool. If you have a sore throat, don't be tempted by ice cream. It is full of sugar and will give you the chills.

Not only is it efficient at warding off vampires, but garlic is great for fighting viruses and giving a boost to your immune system, as well. You must eat it raw, though. Try chopping it finely or mushing it up and sticking it on a slice of buttered toast. You may have heard that chicken soup helps to cure illnesses, but it is not really a wonder drug. Nonetheless, as a fluid it provides you with water; its warmth can soothe your throat; its combination of fats and spices can loosen up stuffed-up noses and clogged-up passages; and a bit of salt can keep you from feeling light-headed.

"But Mom!" whined Sophie, from between the folds of the down quilt. "I don't want any more tea! I keep having to go to the bathroom and then I miss good stuff on TV!"

"Now, dear," said Mrs. Suco. "You know that the doctor said that you need to drink plenty of liquids. And he recommended this tea made from an herb called astragalus. It is supposed to be very good at fighting viruses and will leave you feeling more energetic as well. Doctor Paul said that in China people have been using it for centuries."

"Well, that is fascinating, Mom, but I want to take some real medicine," said Sophie, glaring at her mother. "When Murray Singleton had a cold last month, his mom bought him that lemon

Herbal teas provide relief from a sore throat.

flavored stuff that the cute dog wears around its neck in the TV commercial. He also got to take those cool capsules with the tiny, pretty-colored beads. On TV, they say that taking them will make your cold disappear overnight."

"Did Murray Singleton's cold disappear overnight?"

Sophie scowled at her mother. "Ummm . . . I don't remember."

"Well?" pressed Mrs. Suco. "Did it?"

"I don't think so . . . " mumbled Sophie reluctantly. "But I bet that lemon stuff sure tasted better than the health gook you give me!"

"Sophie, are you feeling better this evening than you were this morning?" demanded Mrs. Suco.

"Well, what with all that healthy zinc and echiwhatever and astro-whatever you keep giving me . . . yeah, I guess so," admitted Sophie reluctantly. "Only I wish you would buy me some of that cough syrup you used to get from the drugstore when I was little."

"But Sophie, you don't have a cough."

"Yeah, I know. But last night I didn't sleep well. And I remember that whenever I took that cough syrup, it used to make me really sleepy."

"Well, that's not very good for you. Those cough syrups contain antihistamines that can make you very tired. But luckily for you, Doctor Paul advised me to buy some chamomile tea. He

said it's wonderfully calming and helps people get to sleep without any chemicals."

"Oh great," groaned Sophie. "More natural stuff."

Drugstore Remedies

As you are probably aware from all of the ads in magazines, TV commercials, and the pill-packed aisles in your local pharmacy, there are hundreds of syrups, tablets, sprays, gel caps, drops, lotions, and potions all claiming to ease your aches, soothe your pain, and cure your cold or flu. You might be confused about which of these many brightly-colored packages is the right one for you. Make sure you and your parents read the packages carefully so that you can match the proper medicine to the symptoms you are experiencing:

If You Want to . . .	Choose a Medicine with . . .
a) Unclog a stuffed-up nose and breathe more easily	a) Nasal decongestant
b) Loosen mucus so you can cough it up	b) Expectorant
c) Ease your cough	c) Cough suppressant
d) Stop sneezing and a runny nose	d) Antihistamine
e) Relieve fever, headaches, minor aches	e) Analgesic (pain relievers)

For the pharmaceutical companies that make them, these over-the-counter remedies are a big business—four billion dollars' worth a year (just for colds). However, it is a mistake to believe that any of these medicines "cure" colds or flu, or even help you to get better more quickly. What they do is ease, or hide, the cold and flu symptoms. Some doctors believe that such medications can actually prolong your illness because it is the symptoms themselves—sneezing, coughing, a runny nose—that help your body fight the infection. Masking your symptoms not only undermines this process, but it also lulls you into believing that you are ready to get out of bed and rock 'n' roll—when in fact, you aren't.

If you do decide to use over-the-counter drugs to help you feel better, you or your parents should ask your doctor which he or she recommends. There have been some reports that decongestants can produce hallucinations and irritability. And although analgesics—acetaminophen (such as Tylenol) and ibuprofen (such as Motrin) are the most common—really do relieve fevers and aches, avoid aspirin, which will put you at risk of developing Reye's syndrome, a serious illness that can be a complication of the flu.

Because antibiotics don't work on viruses, they can't cure either colds or flu. For flu, doctors can prescribe a medicine (either amantadine or rimantadine) that can reduce the length of the illness. However, both of these medicines only work if you take them within forty-eight

Steam can help to unclog blocked nasal passages.

hours of the flu symptoms' appearance. Also, they are only effective in fighting the Type A virus. Because they can produce unpleasant side effects, doctors usually prescribe this medicine only for people who risk developing severe complications from the flu.

How Steam Can Help

Viruses thrive in hot, dry atmospheres. This is why wintertime—when you are cooped up with many people in small, overheated spaces—is such a favorite time for both colds and flu viruses. To make viruses' mission more difficult, and yours (to stay healthy) easier—get your parents to invest in a humidifier. A humidifier is a small, quiet machine that sprays a fine, cool mist into

30408000000576

the air. Not only does it help to keep viruses at bay, it also relieves sore throats and stuffy noses.

Similarly, a hot, steamy bath or shower, or a bowl filled with hot water (breathe in the steam by standing over the bowl with a towel over your head) is great for unclogging your nasal passages.

Natural Remedies

Because no over-the-counter pharmaceutical remedy has succeeded in curing either colds or the flu, more and more Americans have been discovering—and rediscovering—the very real benefits of natural remedies derived from medicinal plants, minerals, and herbs.

The most tried, true, and traditional of these is vitamin C. Although you can get it naturally in oranges, lemons, limes, and grapefruits, taking extra tablets once you feel yourself coming down with something can really do wonders. Some studies have shown that taking 1,000 mg of vitamin C per day not only cuts both the length of your illness and the severity of your symptoms in half, but also reduces the risk of secondary infections.

More recently (re)discovered are the incredible benefits of zinc. Taking up to 100 to 120 mg a day of this mineral, for the first two or three days that you are sick, has been shown to cut the length and severity of your illness in half. The sooner you begin, the more amazing the results. It has been proven that the most effective way to

Many people find natural remedies—those derived from plants, minerals, and herbs—to be beneficial.

take zinc is in lozenges. In fact, sucking on a 30 mg zinc tablet is just like sucking on a cough drop or throat lozenge. So as soon as you feel the first tinglings or itchings of a sore throat, try out a zinc lozenge.

Equally popular of late is the herb echinacea, commonly known as the coneflower. Until a few years ago, the powerful healing attributes of this purplish-colored prairie wildflower were known only to Native Americans. Today, however, its roots, seeds, juice, and flowerheads are made into capsules, extracts, and teas that toughen your immune system and have proven especially good at fighting cold and flu viruses. Like the remedies mentioned above, it is best to take echinacea—four to five dropfuls of extract (or 900 mg) a day—as soon as your symptoms appear.

Cat's claw and astragalus are two other herbs that are great at helping to fight off viruses. Elderberry is especially brutal when it comes head-to-head with both Type A and B flu viruses, and both licorice root and stinging nettle are known to be tough on flu viruses as well. Meanwhile, if you want natural relief from coughing and sore throats, try mullein, marshmallow root, slippery elm bark, or the leaves of the bananalike plantain. All of these herbs contain thick substances that coat and soothe irritated respiratory passages and make you feel better. All should be available at any health food store.

Some of these remedies—raw garlic? purple flowers? slippery elm bark?—might seem a little far-fetched to you. At least they are scientifically proven. Not so many decades ago, there were people who swore that sniffing baked pumpkin seeds would clear a stuffed-up nose, and those who would place frogs in bags around their necks in order to get rid of a cough.

The next time you're laid up in bed, feeling ridiculous because your dad has you hunched over a bowl of steaming water scented with eucalyptus leaves, consider this: not so long ago there were folks who used to try to cure their colds by planting a big juicy kiss on the head of . . . a mouse!

Glossary

analgesic   Pain relieving medicine.

antibiotics   Natural substances produced by microorganisms used to kill other disease-causing bacteria.

antibodies   Proteins made by the body's immune system that fight viruses.

bronchitis   Serious infection of the bronchi (tubes leading to the lungs).

contagious   Disease or virus that is communicable by contact.

contaminate   To infect.

epidemic   Outbreak (of a disease) that affects a great many people in a region.

fatigue   Tiredness.

gastroenteritis   Viral infection, also known as stomach flu, that attacks the stomach and intestines.

humidifier Machine that sprays fine drops of water into the air.

mucus Fluid-like substance produced by your nasal passages that expels viruses.

nausea Feeling of queasiness that usually precedes vomiting.

pandemic Outbreak that occurs over a wide geographic area and affects an extremely high proportion of the population.

pneumonia Disease of the lungs characterized by inflammation, which is caused by infection or irritants.

symptoms Physical signs or clues that let you (and your doctor) know that you are sick.

vaccine Tiny quantity of a virus (usually dead) that, injected into your system, triggers your body into making antibodies that fight the real virus.

virus Tiny microorgansims that, growing and multiplying in living cells, spread diseases.

Where to Go for Help

In the United States

Centers for Disease Control and Prevention (CDC)
1600 Clifton Road, MS D-25
Atlanta, GA 30333
(404) 639-3286
(800) 311-3435
Web site: http://www.cdc.gov

Food and Drug Administration (FDA)
Department of Health and Human Services
5600 Fishers Lane
Rockville, MD 20857
(888) INFO-FDA [463-6332]
Web site: http://www.fda.gov

Herb Research Foundation
1007 Pearl Street, Suite 200
Boulder, CO 80302
(303) 449-2265
(800) 748-2617
Web site: http://www.herbs.org

National Institute of Allergies and Infectious
    Diseases (NIAID)
Office of Communications and Public Liaison
Building 31, Room 7A-50
31 Center Drive MSC 2520
Bethesda, MD 20892-2520
Web site: http://www.niaid.nih.gov

National Institutes of Health (NIH)
Visitor Information Center
Bethesda, MD 20892
(301) 496-1776
Web site: http://www.nih.gov

In Canada

Canadian Herb Society (CHS)
5251 Oak Street
Vancouver, BC V6M 4H1
(604) 224-0457
Web site: http://www.herbsociety.ca

Laboratory Centre for Disease Control
Health Canada Bureau of Infectious Diseases
Tunney's Pasture
Ottawa, ON, K1A 0L2
Web site: http://hwcweb.hwc.ca/hpb/lcdc/new_e.html

Web Sites

KidsHealth by the Nemours Foundation
http://www.kidshealth.org

National Influenza Immunization Campaign
http://www.fightflu.com

World Health Organization (WHO)
http://www.who.int

For Further Reading

Feinstein, Alice. *Prevention's Healing With Vitamins: The Most Effective Vitamin and Mineral Treatments for Everyday Health Problems and Serious Disease.* Emmaus, PA: Rodale Press, 1998.

Finley, Bryce. *Echinacea: How to Grow, Harvest, and Use This Amazing Flower to Fight Colds, Flu, and Infection by Boosting Your Immune System.* Tucson, AZ: Brycefinley, 1996.

Heinrichs, Jay and Dorothy B. Heinrichs. *Home Remedies from the Country Doctor.* Emmaus, PA: Rodale Press, 1999.

Levinson, David and Laura Gaccione. *Health and Illness: A Cross-Cultural Encyclopedia.* Santa Barbara, CA: ABC-Clio, 1997.

MacFarlane, Muriel K. *The Sinus Handbook: A Self-Help Guide.* Chicago, IL: United Research Publishers, 1997.

O'Neill, Hugh (Editor). *The Doctor's Book of Home Remedies for Preventing Disease: Tips and Techniques so Powerful They Stop Diseases before They Start.* Emmaus, PA: Rodale Press, 1999.

Powell, Don R. *The American Institute for Preventive Medicine's Self-Care: Your Family Guide to Symptoms and how to Treat Them.* Austin, TX: Peoples Medical Society, 1996.

Ullman, Robert. *Homeopathic Self-Care: A Quick and Easy Guide for the Whole Family.* Rocklin, CA: Prima Communications, 1999.

Index

63

About the Author

Mick Isle has a degree in journalism from Trinity College in Dublin, Ireland.

Photo Credits

Cover image by Ira Fox. All interior shots by Maura Boruchow except p. 2 by Brian Silak; p. 12 © Custom Medical; pp. 21, 31 by Ira Fox; p. 39 © Scott Camazine/Photo Researchers, Inc.

Layout

Geri Giordano